THE ROMAN NEWS

ANDREW LANGLEY & PHILIP DE SOUZA

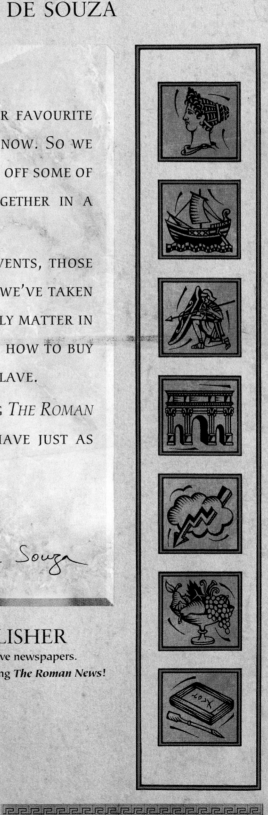

DEAR READER,

THE ROMAN NEWS HAS BEEN YOUR FAVOURITE DAILY PAPER FOR HUNDREDS OF YEARS, NOW. SO WE THOUGHT IT WAS ABOUT TIME WE DUSTED OFF SOME OF OUR BEST STORIES AND PUT THEM TOGETHER IN A SPECIAL EDITION — AND HERE IT IS!

WE'VE REPORTED ON KEY NEWS EVENTS, THOSE THAT CAUSED A STIR AT THE TIME. AND WE'VE TAKEN A FRESH LOOK AT THE THINGS THAT REALLY MATTER IN LIFE — SPORT, FASHION, FEASTING, EVEN HOW TO BUY YOURSELF AN HONEST, HARD-WORKING SLAVE.

WE'VE HAD A GREAT TIME PUTTING THE ROMAN NEWS TOGETHER, AND WE HOPE YOU HAVE JUST AS MUCH FUN READING IT!

THE EDITORS-IN-CHIEF

Andrew Langley   Philip de Souza

A NOTE FROM OUR PUBLISHER

As we all know, the Ancient Romans didn't really have newspapers.
But if they had, we're sure they would all have been reading **The Roman News**!
We hope you enjoy it.

Walker Books

WALKER BOOKS
AND SUBSIDIARIES
LONDINIUM · BOSTON · SYDNEY

CONTENTS

MAP OF THE ROMAN EMPIRE

Hadrian's Wall

BRITAIN

GERMANY

FRANCE

THE ALPS

River Tiber

Rome

SPAIN

CORSICA

Ostia
Alba
Longa
Pompeii

New
Carthage

SARDINIA

ITALY

GREECE

Black Sea

TURKEY

SYRIA

CYPRUS

NORTH AFRICA

Carthage
Zama

SICILY

Mediterranean
Sea

CRETE

EGYPT

Red
Sea

Extent of the Roman Empire
at about AD 200

Map by GILLIAN TYLER

BIRTH OF A GIANT

Illustrated by CHRISTIAN HOOK

OUR GLORIOUS CITY of Rome is today at the heart of a vast and powerful Empire. Yet how many of us know how and when it was founded?

EVEN HERE at *The Roman News*, we cannot discover exactly what happened all those years ago — the story is so ancient that the truth has been lost in the mists of time.

But could there be any better account than that given in popular legend — the dramatic story of the twin brothers, Romulus and Remus?

THROWN OUT TO DIE

As tiny babies, the twins were cruelly taken from their mother and left by the River Tiber to starve.

But miraculously, a wolf saved them from death, and cared for them as if they were her own cubs. Then the boys were discovered

by a shepherd, who took them to his home.

The years passed, and after many adventures the brothers learned that they were of royal blood — princes of a nearby town, Alba Longa.

The twins returned to Alba Longa and claimed back the kingdom. And to celebrate their victory, they decided to build a splendid new town on one of the seven hills by the River Tiber, where the wolf had discovered

POWER STRUGGLE: Romulus and Remus fight for the right to be king.

MOTHERLY LOVE: A wolf saved the twins from death.

them all those years ago.

But which brother was to rule this new town? The twins looked for a sign from the gods.

Remus searched the skies and saw six vultures, but Romulus saw twelve and claimed this gave *him* the right to be king.

A FIGHT TO THE DEATH

The brothers quarrelled and swords were drawn. A bitter fight followed, and Remus fell — stabbed by Romulus!

With his brother dead, Romulus took the throne,

and the new town was given the name Rome in his honour.

Of course, there are people who sneer and say this is just a silly legend. They claim that Romulus never existed.

But these mockers should climb up to the top of the Palatine Hill in Rome, and visit the plain wooden hut where Romulus once lived.

And whatever really did happen all those years ago, we are sure of two things — our city was founded in 753 BC and our first king was called Romulus. ✚

WHAT HAPPENED NEXT?

ROMULUS WAS just the first of many kings to rule Rome as it grew into a large and bustling city.

BUT IN THE END, these kings became far too greedy for power and wealth — they had to go.

In 509 BC, the nobles

drove the last king out of Rome and made the city a republic, in which the leaders were chosen by the people.

Rome thrived and became a rich and busy city. It conquered more and more land until, by the 170s BC, it ruled all of Italy. We were well on the way to becoming the proud and powerful nation of today. ✚

HANNIBAL INVADES

Illustrated by RON TINER

ROME HAS HAD some nasty shocks in its long history. But perhaps the worst was when the Carthaginians invaded in the 200s BC. *The Roman News* looks back at the key events of those terrifying years.

CARTHAGE HAD long been a powerful city, controlling most of the Mediterranean Sea.

But our nation was rapidly growing stronger, and by the middle of the 260s BC, we were locked into deadly combat with the Carthaginians.

The war dragged on for 20 years, with neither side able to overpower the other. Then, in 241 BC, our brave troops won a massive victory.

Furious at this defeat, the Carthaginians swore to crush Rome once and for all. Moving westwards around the North African coast, they crossed to Spain and set up a base called New Carthage.

Here, Spanish troops rushed to join forces with them, tempted by the chance of battle plunder.

The Carthaginians' brilliant young general, Hannibal, quickly built up an army of 40,000 men. To these he added a terrifying weapon — 40 African war elephants, trained to charge at the enemy and trample them.

CROSSING THE MOUNTAINS

Hannibal was ready to invade our homeland. His army marched north, gathering even more men on the way. But then Hannibal reached the icy mountains of the Alps.

RISKY ROUTE: Hannibal's army suffered terrible losses on the march through the Alps.

Luckily for Rome, the mountain passes took their toll. By the time Hannibal reached Italy in 218 BC, a quarter of his troops and many of the elephants had perished.

Yet despite this, Hannibal won three fierce battles against our army, leaving the countryside littered with Roman dead.

THE ENEMY AT THE DOOR

By 216 BC, it seemed certain that disaster would hit Rome. The city was helpless — all Hannibal had to do was march into it.

But Hannibal's next move was a mistake. His army was short of men, and instead of attacking our city, he wasted many years wandering through southern Italy in search of food and extra troops.

Rome used the time to rebuild its army and, in 204 BC, our leaders launched a bold plan.

Under General Scipio, an army of elite Roman troops was sent to Africa, to mount an attack on the city of Carthage itself.

In desperation, the Carthaginians recalled Hannibal and his army. But at Zama, southwest of Carthage, they were totally defeated. And this once powerful nation fell under Rome's control.

Rome had faced the greatest threat in its entire history — and conquered it!

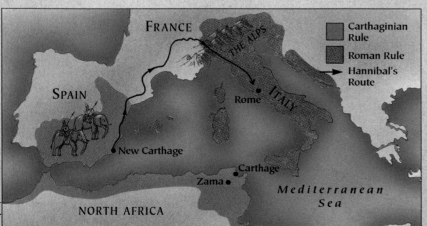

Map by CHRIS FORSEY

FRANCE

THE ALPS

SPAIN

ITALY

Rome

New Carthage

Zama

Carthage

Mediterranean Sea

NORTH AFRICA

Carthaginian Rule

Roman Rule

Hannibal's Route

INVASION: Hannibal's route into Italy took him across the dangerous Alps.

CAESAR STABBED!

Illustrated by P. J. LYNCH

BETRAYED: Julius Caesar is attacked in the Senate House, the very heart of the government.

CAESAR IS DEAD, screamed the front page of *The Roman News* on 15 March, 44 BC. We look back at that shocking event.

ROME WAS IN turmoil after its leader's murder. Caesar had been stabbed to death — by men who were once his friends!

So ended the man who set in motion the greatest change in our nation's history — the shift from a republic, with leaders chosen by the people, to an empire, with one supreme ruler.

Julius Caesar had always wanted power. In 59 BC, he had become consul, the very highest position in the land. But his term as consul only lasted a year, and he did not want to give up power.

So Caesar made a deal with two powerful friends, Pompey and Crassus. They agreed to control the Republic of Rome between the three of them.

But Crassus died soon afterwards, and by 49 BC Caesar and Pompey were at each other's throats, fighting one another for control of the Republic.

Caesar was backed by loyal troops, though — the men who had fought beside him to conquer vast areas of France. And it didn't take them long to smash Pompey's army.

I THOUGHT YOU WERE MY FRIENDS

Cartoon by MARTIN BROWN

Nothing could stop Caesar now. Soon he was made sole leader of the Republic — *for life*.

But his popularity didn't last. Some people feared that he wanted to make himself king. And the people of Rome had vowed they would never accept another, after throwing the last king out 500 years earlier.

So a group of senators, Caesar's fellow politicians, decided to kill him and take power back into their own hands.

On that fateful March morning, the plotters surrounded Caesar in the Senate House and plunged their daggers into his body. Then they fled, waving their bloody knives in triumph.

But the plotters did not escape. They were hunted down by Caesar's adopted son and heir, who took control of the government himself.

This man, Augustus Caesar, was to become the first in the long line of emperors who have ruled us ever since.

Julius Caesar's over-powering ambition had brought him death, but it had brought us the Roman Empire.

CITY DESTROYED

Illustrated by ALAN FRASER

NO ESCAPE: People flee from the volcano's deadly hail of stones and ash.

LUCKY ESCAPE!

ON THAT FATEFUL DAY, writer Pliny the Younger was just 30 kilometres away, in the town of Misenum. Here is his first-hand account of fleeing from the disaster.

"WE SAW THE SEA sucked away and forced back by the earthquake. It had shrunk away from the shore, and many sea creatures were stranded on dry land.

Ashes were already falling, not as yet very thickly. I looked around — a dense black cloud was coming up behind us, spreading over the earth like a flood.

'Let us leave the road while we can still see,' I said, 'or we shall be knocked down and trampled underfoot in the dark.'

We had scarcely sat down when absolute darkness fell — not the dark of a moonless or cloudy night, but as if a lamp had been put out in a closed room.

You could hear the loud shrieks of women, the wailing of children, and the shouting of men.

A curious kind of light appeared, not daylight but more like the light of a distant fire.

Then darkness came on once more and ashes began to fall again, this time in heavy showers.

We rose from time to time and shook them off, otherwise we would have been buried and crushed beneath their weight.

At last, there was genuine daylight. We were terrified to see that everything was changed, buried deep in ashes like snowdrifts."

MOUNT VESUVIUS is peaceful enough today, with its olive groves and grazing animals. Yet it was the cause of one of the worst disasters ever to hit our nation — the death of an entire town.

IN THE AFTERNOON of 24 August, AD 79, Mount Vesuvius turned into a killer.

The volcano erupted, spewing out vast clouds of ash and stones, and thick black smoke. The burning ash rained down on the bustling town of Pompeii, just 10 kilometres away.

Choking and blinded by the smoke, people fled in terror, barely able to run as an earthquake shook the ground.

Within hours, the ash had buried all but the tallest buildings.

More than 20,000 people died that day, smothered by the ash. A once-thriving town had vanished!

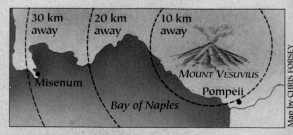

FALLOUT: The spread of ash from the volcano.

VICTORY VISION

A remarkable sight was seen at the Battle of the Milvian Bridge. A Christian symbol had been painted on the shield of every single one of Constantine's soldiers.

The Emperor was told in a dream to fight under this sign. And now he claims it helped him win.

HOLY WAR: No hope for Maxentius' troops, as Constantine's army storms to victory.

ONE RULER!

Illustrated by TONY SMITH

HISTORY HAS SHOWN that our Empire thrives when one strong leader is in control. But by the AD 300s, the Empire was split among several squabbling rulers. Then one man grasped the reins of power — the Emperor Constantine.

THE TROUBLE had all begun in AD 285, when the Emperor Diocletian split our Empire into four separate areas, each ruled by a different man.

Constantine first came to power 21 years later, in AD 306, as the ruler of one of these areas.

Although he controlled Germany, France and Britain, this was not enough for Constantine. He vowed to destroy his three co-emperors and become the sole ruler.

First, he had to seize control of the city of Rome from Maxentius, one of his co-emperors.

ON THE ATTACK

Gathering together his battle-hardened army, Constantine swept down through France, arriving in Italy in AD 312.

Maxentius fled, rather than face the invaders. But Constantine caught up with him near Rome's Milvian Bridge, where a flimsy row of linked boats spanned the River Tiber. Here, Constantine's army won a decisive battle.

Maxentius and his men tried to flee over the bridge of boats, but most of them drowned when the bridge collapsed.

Constantine marched triumphantly into Rome and set about planning his next move.

His main rival was now Licinius, who had already defeated the remaining co-emperor, Maximinus.

In AD 324, Constantine attacked Licinius and, after two fierce battles, crushed his rival's army.

At last, our Empire was safely back in the firm hands of a single, strong ruler.

NO PEACE

CONSTANTINE CAME to power at a time of great turmoil for the Empire. Back in AD 324, *The Roman News* took a long hard look at the problems, and highlighted some of the troubles we faced.

■ For the last 200 years, our lands have been under continual attack from the fierce barbarian tribes who live outside our borders.

But the Empire is now so big that we simply can't protect all our lands. One day, these tribes will break through and ruin us.

■ It's no longer the politicians in Rome who decide who'll be emperor. The army is so powerful that now it's the soldiers who choose our leader. And if the one they pick doesn't come up to scratch, they kill him and choose another!

So emperors come and go, and none rules long enough to sort out the chaos in the Empire. In AD 238, we had seven emperors in just one year.

■ Most of the soldiers aren't even Romans. Citizens don't want to join the army any more, and it's cheaper to pay barbarians to fight for us — even though these foreigners could turn against us at any time.

COLOSSEUM OPENS

Illustrated by CHRISTIAN HOOK

IT'S THE MOST famous and most popular place in Rome — it's the Colosseum! Here, *The Roman News* remembers the spectacular celebrations that were held when this fabulous sports arena first opened in AD 80.

THE COLOSSEUM took more than ten years to build, but it was worth waiting for. The opening celebrations went on for 100 days.

By mid-morning each day the seats were full, as citizens and slaves crowded into the stands. The poorest sat right at the top, while the seats closest to the arena were for senators and other important people.

Day after day the arena sands were soaked with blood, as pairs of gladiators hacked each other to death.

Other gladiators pitted their wits against exotic wild animals — lions, leopards, panthers and bears. More than 9,000 animals were brought from all corners of the Empire to be slaughtered.

Spectators gasped as gladiators appeared as if by magic on the arena floor — hoisted up by cranes from the network of tunnels below.

WATERY WONDERS

But the highlight of the entire celebrations was the flooding of the arena for an amazingly realistic naval battle.

Ship fought against ship, ramming each other until the lake was littered with sinking vessels and drowning rowers.

But all these marvels just marked the start of the Colosseum's years of glory. It has hosted thousands of gladiator fights since its opening, attracting huge audiences week after week.

Of course, there are many other fine games arenas throughout our Empire. Nearly every important city has one. But none can compare with the Colosseum in Rome — it's still the biggest and the best! ✠

KILL OR BE KILLED: A Retiarius (left) and a Hoplomachus clash in a battle to the death.

Illustrated by KATHERINE BAXTER

COLOSSAL COLOSSEUM: Seating for 50,000 people.

INTO THE ARENA

Illustrated by CHRISTIAN HOOK

WHAT BOY hasn't dreamed of being a gladiator? We all know they're only slaves and criminals — but they're still fascinating! Here's what one seasoned fighter has to say about life in the arena.

I'VE BEEN a gladiator for ten months now, and believe me that's good going. None of the other gladiators I trained with is still alive.

You only get a few months' training, and that's just with wooden weapons — if we had proper ones, we'd attack the guards and run for it!

IN COMBAT: A Retiarius tries to net a Thracian.

You can't choose which kind of gladiator to be, but each of the three main types has its good points and its bad.

The Retiarius' major advantage is his net — he uses it to tangle up his opponent. But if you can get his net off him, then he's only got a long trident. And that's so big and heavy, it's useless.

The Thracian has a small shield. But although it's light, and allows him to be quick on his feet, it doesn't give him any protection. He has a good long dagger, though.

I was lucky enough to be trained as a Samnite. I'm quite well protected, with a huge shield and a strong helmet. I've no chest armour, though — so if a stab gets past my shield to my stomach, I'm a goner.

I remember my first fight — I was terrified! But with slaves using leather whips and red-hot irons to force you into the arena, you don't hang around for long.

I've lasted five fights now — four more than most. Mind you, I only survived the last one because the crowd gave the thumbs up, showing it wanted me to live.

I just hope the crowd goes on supporting me. Then, maybe one day I'll be rewarded with my freedom. ➦

FIVE THINGS YOU DIDN'T KNOW ABOUT GLADIATORS

I The first recorded gladiator games were in 264 BC, at the funeral of a nobleman.

II A gladiator called Spartacus led a slave revolt in 73 BC. It took two years for the Roman army to defeat him.

III Publius Ostorius of Pompeii was the longest-surviving gladiator — he lasted for 51 fights.

IV The biggest-ever games were held by the Emperor Trajan at the Colosseum in AD 107. More than 10,000 gladiators and 10,000 animals died.

V At one time, women fought as gladiators. This was banned in AD 200. ➦

ARMED TO THE TEETH: A Samnite geared up and ready for a fight.

A DAY AT THE RACES

Illustrated by ANGUS McBRIDE

FIRST PAST THE POST: Charioteers lash their horses in a desperate race for the finishing line.

IS CHARIOT-RACING a waste of time? After all, at least 400,000 people spend one day a week just at the racecourses in Rome. *The Roman News* asked one regular racegoer — what's the appeal?

❓ Some people call the races a "childish passion". Do you agree?
Well, I don't know about childish, but they certainly make you passionate! By the time the chariots — anything from four to twelve of them — shoot out of the starting gates, I'm already shouting for my team. By the third lap, I'm wishing my charioteer would lash his horses even harder.

Then it's the seventh lap — the horses go flat out for the finishing line, and the whole crowd is on its feet, screaming.

❓ Don't some people get a bit carried away?
Well, yes, I suppose the younger lads get rather over-excited, and fights can spill onto the streets.

But it's just because everyone wants their favourite team to win. I support the Greens, but all four teams have devoted fans — some people go for the Blues, the Reds or the Whites.

❓ What about the dangers on the track?
Chariots are pushed on to the walls sometimes, then they tip over or their wheels smash. And because the drivers have the reins looped around their waists, many of them can't avoid being dragged beneath the hooves and wheels of other racers.

❓ But you don't think a day at the races is a waste of time?
No, I definitely don't! And neither do thousands of others. After all, there are five racecourses in Rome alone, and most cities around the Empire have at least one of their own.

Let's face it, chariot-racing is here to stay! ◙

GOOD SLAVE GUIDE

Illustrated by MAXINE HAMIL

YOU'RE JUST ABOUT to set up house — and no home is complete without slaves. But how do you choose and buy them? By taking *The Roman News'* advice, of course!

FIRSTLY, how many slaves will you need? Well, if you're rich, you can own as many as you like. A wealthy family may have up to 500 to run all its houses and farms, and some emperors have had as many as 20,000 slaves.

But let's assume you're more of a typical case — you'll want at least five or six slaves.

Next, you'll have to decide exactly what sort of slaves to buy. It's worth paying extra for a few highly trained people — a cook, a tailor and maybe a secretary.

Then you'll want a strong man for all the heavy work, and some attractive young slaves to serve your guests at dinner parties.

Now for the tricky part. Which are the best kinds of slave?

We advise buying the children of other slaves, even if they cost more. They've grown up in slavery and they've been working since they could walk, so they don't know any other way of life.

Alternatively, you could try children whose parents have abandoned them. These youngsters won't cost you anything, and there are plenty of places around town where they are left. Bring them up as part of the family, and you'll find that they're very loyal.

But remember. If these children can ever prove that their parents weren't slaves, then you won't be able to keep them.

Sometimes you can buy prisoners-of-war, though often they don't speak Latin, or criminals who've lost their freedom as a punishment. Both kinds can be cheap — so see what's on offer at your local market.

NO FREEDOM FOR SLAVES

One last word of warning. Some people allow their slaves to keep any tips they're given, so that they can eventually buy their freedom. We urge you not to do this, as you'll only have to buy and train yet more slaves.

HARD-WEARING: Strong, fit slaves are useful for the hundreds of heavy jobs around the house and garden.

THEY RISK THEIR LIVES

Illustrated by PETER MORTER

WE ALL PRAISE the bravery of our soldiers and admire the nerve of our gladiators, but what about the courage of our traders? The life of a merchant isn't all plain sailing, you know!

WHETHER THEY travel over land or sea, our merchants are away from their families for months, even years, at a time.

And whenever they set out on an expedition, they risk their lives for us.

Pirates, ambush and shipwreck are just some of the dangers that these brave men have to face on our behalf.

To bring back the luxurious silks and exotic spices that we value so highly, our traders must either cross the gruelling deserts of Asia to China, or undertake the difficult journey by ship down the Red Sea to distant India.

And it's not just these long-distance trips that are so perilous. The merchants that sail on the Mediterranean Sea also face dangers that all too often prove fatal.

Every year, hundreds of ships are wrecked on the rocky Mediterranean coastline. And there are pirates everywhere.

If traders are attacked, it's not just their cargo they risk losing, but their freedom. If they survive capture by pirates, they face a life of slavery.

GROWING CITIES NEED FOOD

So why do our merchants continue to make these hazardous journeys?

Well, it's not just for the money they make by bringing in luxury goods.

The food they import stops people starving. So many of us now live in cities that our farmers can't grow enough crops to feed everyone.

Where would we be without the grain harvest from Egypt, or the cargoes of wine from France and olive oil from Spain?

So the next time you sit down to dinner, spare a thought for those who risk their lives to put the food on your plate.

WOOL, GEMS AND SLAVES *from Britain*

WINE AND SLAVES *from France*

SLAVES AND IRON *from Germany*

SLAVES *from around the Caspian Sea*

CARPETS *from Turkey*

SILK *from China* →

OLIVE OIL, SILVER, GOLD AND LEAD *from Spain*

Rome

Mediterranean Sea

SLAVES AND HONEY *from Greece*

PERFUME *from Iran*

GRAIN, MARBLE AND PURPLE DYE *from Tunisia*

GRAIN, SLAVES AND LINEN *from Egypt*

GLASSWARE AND SLAVES *from Syria*

N

SPICES AND GEMS *from India*

EUROPE   **ASIA**

CHINA

INDIA

AFRICA

Red Sea

W   **E**

S

WORLDWIDE TRADE: Merchants travel to every point of the compass, returning with essential supplies as well as luxury goods.

PORTUS AT A PRICE

WAREHOUSES FOR RENT

SUPERB LOCATION!
Situated in the greatest harbour in the Empire, these buildings provide ample storage space for cargoes of oil, grain, timber or wine.

HISTORIC HARBOUR!
Begun by the Emperor Claudius in about AD 50, Portus is now the busiest port in the world.

SAFETY FIRST!
A lighthouse at the entrance burns 24 hours a day, guiding hundreds of ships to the harbour.

CAPITAL CONNECTIONS!
A regular riverboat service links Portus to Rome — just 30 kilometres up the River Tiber. Journey time is a matter of hours.

For more details of this terrific opportunity, contact
**THE GUILD OF SHIPPING MERCHANTS,
BEHIND THE THEATRE, OSTIA**

PIRATE ATTACK!

JUST THE WORD "pirate" is enough to strike terror into the heart of any trader. But what's it really like to be attacked by these bloodthirsty raiders? *The Roman News* spoke to a lucky survivor…

❓ Tell us about that fateful day.

Well, I was a passenger on a small merchant ship, sailing from Tunisia to Sicily. There were ten of us on board — three other merchants besides myself, and a crew of six.

On our first day at sea I noticed a small galley coming towards us. As it drew closer, my heart sank. It was a pirate ship!

❓ What did you do?

There was nothing we could do. The coastline was too rocky to land, and there wasn't enough wind to fill our sails. The galley had oars, so it could easily outrun us. The pirates had planned their attack well.

❓ So what happened?

The pirates drew up alongside our ship and jumped on board. There must have been about 50 of them — all armed to the teeth with daggers, swords and spears. It was terrifying. I really thought I was going to die.

❓ How ever did you get out alive?

I quickly realized the pirates didn't want our cargo — they wanted us! We were herded on board their ship like animals. One of our crew tried to fight back, but the pirates beat him so badly that he nearly died. Then they locked us in the ship's dark, smelly hold, with no food and only one bucket of water.

And when we reached the next port, we were sold as slaves.

❓ But I believe you had a lucky escape?

I certainly did! A fellow merchant spotted me and he managed to buy me back. I don't know when I'll be able to repay him, but one thing's for sure — I'm never going to sea again!

EMPIRE OR REPUBLIC?

Illustrated by CHRISTIAN HOOK

LED BY A SINGLE RULER, the Roman Empire has soared to new heights of power and success — or so some people say. Others think life was better before the Empire, when our nation was a republic. Here, *The Roman News* examines both points of view.

SUPPORTERS OF THE Republic point out that back in those days, power wasn't just in the hands of one man, the emperor.

Instead, Rome was governed by 600 senators, chosen from only the wealthy families.

They were led by two consuls, who could never become too greedy or powerful because they only ruled for one year. Then they were replaced by two new consuls.

In Republican times, all citizens (free men — not women or slaves, of course) could take part in running our nation.

For a start, citizens could choose the senators and consuls. They could also go to the Forum or to the Field of Mars in the city of Rome, to hear politicians' speeches.

And afterwards, they could vote on important matters, such as whether or not to go to war.

A CHANGE FOR THE BETTER

But of course everything changed after the great Augustus became Rome's first emperor in 27 BC.

Nowadays, it is the emperor who governs our nation and makes all the important decisions.

Some people claim that he has too much power. But these critics forget that it was the emperors who made our nation the greatest in the world — winning vast areas of new land for us and protecting us against foreign invaders.

Besides, even the most powerful emperor can't rule if the people turn against him — his very life may be in danger if he becomes too unpopular.

A MIGHTY MAN:
Augustus, our first emperor.

That's why emperors are so keen to keep us happy. They pay out huge sums of money to give us free food and entertainments — from gladiator games to the Triumphs held after great battles.

Here at *The Roman News*, there's no doubt in our minds. Under the emperors, life has been happier, safer and more glorious. Long live the Roman Empire! ◻

VESPASIAN'S TRIUMPH

Illustrated by RICHARD HOOK

EVERY ROMAN LOVES a good show. And one of the very best was the victory parade given by the Emperor Vespasian in AD 71. *The Roman News'* reporter was at the scene...

THE STREETS of Rome had been packed with crowds since before dawn. And every single building that lined the route was jammed with people hanging out of the windows.

Towards mid-day loud cheering broke out, as the parade finally came into sight.

In the lead were the senators, followed by row upon row of Vespasian's troops.

DAY OF GLORY: The Emperor Vespasian celebrates his victory in Palestine with a magnificent Triumph.

Some were laden with glorious treasures from the battle. Others led the hundreds of sacrificial oxen. These would be slaughtered at the Temple of Jupiter, in thanks for our great victory against the Hebrews, in Palestine.

PRISONERS IN CHAINS

The crowd roared with approval as a litter appeared, on which the enemy leaders were displayed. Behind It came columns of their men in chains.

Then the Emperor himself came into view, and everyone went wild with excitement.

In his purple and gold robes, with his arms and face painted red, Vespasian looked just like Jupiter's statue in the Temple.

As is the custom, the slave who held up Vespasian's crown whispered to him all day long: "Remember that you are only a man." But the roar of the crowd was more than enough to tell the Emperor that to us, he is a god! ✦

FOUR TIPS FOR THE TOP

HOW CAN I GET ahead in life? This question has been asked by hundreds of our readers over the years. Here, to help you, is the advice of *The Roman News'* political editor.

❓ What's the key to political success?
Well, you certainly won't get anywhere in life unless you're a citizen. Being a free man means you can wear a toga, and enjoy the respect that this brings.

However, if you're a slave who's been set free, you won't count fully as a citizen. Only your grandchildren will.

❓ Will it matter if I don't live in the city of Rome itself?
Well, no — it shouldn't. Wherever you live in the Empire, you are still Roman. But men who live in the provinces, away from the city of Rome, can find it more difficult to become successful.

Don't give up hope, though. Remember that General Trajan came from Spain, and he went on to become emperor.

❓ How can I stand out from the ordinary man in the street?
Become a patron, and support poorer citizens. With a crowd of followers swarming around you, you'll look important wherever you go. But it's expensive — if you're to win their support, you'll have to feed and look after all these followers!

❓ What do I need to get started?
That's easy — money! To reach the top, you must first be a senator, in the highest rank of citizens. And to be a senator, you need at least 1,000,000 sestertii — a vast amount, when you think that most soldiers only earn about 3,000 sestertii a year.

Many emperors began as senators, though. So get into the Senate House, and who knows where you might end up! ✦

THE FRONT LINE

Illustrated by ANGUS McBRIDE

HOME SWEET HOME: Legionaries set up camp after a hard day's march.

The rain never stops! It splashes the soldiers' bare legs, drips down their faces and even soaks into their heavy packs.

Although there are mules to carry the tents, each man has to shoulder his own kit. Clothes, bed-roll, food for three days, bucket, pickaxe, stake, saw and digging tools — it's a heavy load.

Each legionary also has to carry his iron helmet and his weapons — a sword and shield, and a pair of javelins — and wear all of his body armour as well.

No wonder the men are so glad to stop and make camp, even though it means more hard work.

Some soldiers stand guard, while others dig a ditch around a square campsite. Then a fence of sharpened stakes is put up inside the ditch, to keep the enemy out.

When this is done, there's a meal of bacon, cheese, dry biscuits and sour wine — then bed.

Tomorrow, it's another 30-kilometre march, and another step closer to Rome's great dream — to conquer the world!

OUR VAST Empire was won by ordinary foot soldiers. In their honour, *The Roman News* reprints an article from AD 80, when our troops were conquering lands at the Empire's most northern edge. A reporter joined them on the march.

LEFT, RIGHT! Left, right! The clatter of hobnailed sandals echoes in my ears as a vast column of soldiers tramps onwards in perfect time. Each day's march brings us another 30 kilometres closer to the enemy. For this is frontier country, the very edge of the known world — the chilly wastes of Britain.

I've joined a legion of 5,000 foot soldiers. These legionaries are grouped into centuries, units of about 80 soldiers. And a group of six centuries makes a cohort — one of ten cohorts in a legion.

The commander of the legion is the great General Agricola. His mission is to conquer the Celtic tribes of northern Britain, and to claim new land for the Empire.

The men march behind their legion's flag with pride — despite the harsh and difficult conditions.

Cartoon by MARTIN BROWN

WELCOME TO BRITAIN

TRIUMPH OF TRAINING: Although fierce, the Celts are no match for our soldiers.

INTO BATTLE

WHILE OUR INTREPID reporter was with the legion in AD 80, he witnessed a fierce battle between our brave soldiers and one of the Celtic tribes. He sent back this account…

THE ENEMY WARRIORS were a terrifying sight. With painted bodies and spiky hair, they raced down the hill towards us, whirling their swords above their heads and screaming battle cries.

Showing their usual impressive battle tactics, our legionaries walked forward in a straight line to confront the Celts.

Our troops stayed close together, in total silence, as they waited for their officers' commands.

CLOSING IN FOR THE KILL

When the Celts were close enough, the order came to attack. Our men raised their javelins and hurled them at the enemy. The long iron spears smashed into shields and bodies.

Then a new order was barked out, and the legionaries broke into a trot. Drawing their short swords, they closed in on the enemy and began stabbing and slashing.

The barbarians fought back bravely. But in the end they turned and ran, leaving dozens of dead and wounded.

Although our troops had won the day, with an enemy as fierce as the Celts more battles are certain to lie ahead.

But today I witnessed Roman discipline and courage at first-hand. And I have no doubts at all that eventually victory will be ours.

KEEP OUT!

Illustrated by ALAN FRASER

CAPTURING NEW land is tough enough, but holding on to it can be even trickier. *The Roman News* reports on the huge defences built to keep the barbarians out of our Empire.

DESPITE THEIR victories in battle, our troops were unable to subdue all of the Celtic tribes in the far north of Britain. So, in AD 122, Emperor Hadrian ordered work to start on a thick stone wall that would stretch for 120 kilometres across the country, to hold back these fierce tribes.

The wall took more than eight years to build, but at 5 metres high, it now reaches to three times the height of the average legionary!

Today, this wall is patrolled night and day. While they are on duty, the soldiers live in one of the 80 turrets, known as Milecastles, built into the wall at intervals along its length.

In addition to the turrets, a series of large forts lies beside the wall, serving as the soldiers' main bases.

But Hadrian's Wall isn't the longest barrier in the Empire. This record is held by a massive defence system built out of wood and earth. It runs for more than 450 kilometres, starting at the Atlantic coast of France and following the northern edge of our Empire.

With defences like these, surely we can all sleep safely.

THE LAST FRONTIER: A Milecastle on Hadrian's Wall.

ROME, A VISITOR'S GUIDE

Illustrated by CHRIS FORSEY

WHEREVER YOU LIVE in the Empire, Rome is the centre of your world. Never been there? Shame on you! Everyone ought to visit Rome at least once. So for all you first-time tourists, *The Roman News* presents an exclusive guide to our capital city.

THERE'S NO better place to start your tour than in the heart of the city, the Roman Forum.

In many ways it's just like a forum in any other important town — an open square surrounded by government buildings, law courts, temples, and the offices of bankers and merchants.

There aren't any of the usual shops and market stalls in the Roman Forum, though.

You'll find these in the nearby Trajan's Forum.

But what you will find are magnificent victory arches and statues put up in honour of our greatest emperors, along with some of Rome's most beautiful stone buildings.

Watch out for the Senate House — if you are lucky, you'll see our nation's leaders hurrying to a meeting there.

There are more sights to see just a short walk away from the Forum. Go east and you'll find the Colosseum, home to thrilling gladiator games. While to the south there is the famous racecourse, the Circus Maximus.

STREET LIFE

The farther you wander from the Forum, the more you'll experience the real flavour of city life.

A word of warning, though — the streets of Rome are colourful, but they can be dangerous! Crumbling blocks of flats can rise as high as six storeys above narrow, dirty streets and alleys.

And the people living there just throw rubbish out of their windows — *and* the contents of their chamberpots. So watch where you put your feet, and keep a weather eye out above you!

Make sure you take good care of your money, too. Sometimes, it seems as if each one of Rome's one million inhabitants is on the streets. The crowds are so thick that robbing people is child's play.

But at least there's less traffic on the roads

THE FORUM: The magnificent business and government buildings of the city's centre.

ELEGANT TOWN HOUSE FOR SALE

Traditional entrance room with ornamental pool, charming dining room, five bedrooms, and large garden with covered walkways and altar to the household gods. Includes many luxury features — central heating, own water supply, kitchen and toilet.

Box No. 9210

IDEAL HOME!

BEAUTIFY YOUR HOME WITH COLOURFUL MOSAIC FLOORING. WE USE THE BEST QUALITY STONE OR GLASS PIECES, LAID INTO A HARD-WEARING PLASTER BASE. PATTERNS OR PICTURES — HUNTING SCENES A SPECIALITY.

THE DECORATORS, BESIDE THE THEATRE OF POMPEY, ROME

COUNTRY COUSINS

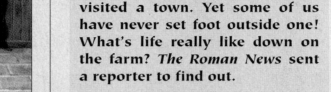

Illustrated by CHRISTIAN HOOK

TIME OFF: Stop at a bar for a rest and a tasty hot snack.

IT'S VERY EASY to mock the country bumpkin who's never visited a town. Yet some of us have never set foot outside one! What's life really like down on the farm? *The Roman News* sent a reporter to find out.

than in many other towns. Most wheeled carts are banned from the city centre during the day.

The bad news is that the nights are filled with the noisy rumble of cartwheels over stone cobbles — you won't get all that much sleep if you stay overnight!

When you need a break from your sight-seeing, pop into a bar for a glass of wine and some tasty soup or stew. There

are lots of bars about — these are where most Romans buy hot meals, as only wealthy families have proper kitchens.

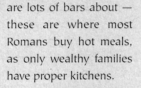

Don't rest for too long, though — in a city as wonderful as Rome, there's always something new and exciting just round the corner, waiting to be discovered.

HERE IN TUSCANY we're three days' travel away from Rome — and it feels like it.

There's hardly a sound, apart from the crowing of cockerels, and the gentle creak of farm carts.

Set on the slopes of a fertile hillside, this estate is a heavenly place to live.

The owner's two-storey villa is as fine as any wealthy family's town house. The large rooms are decorated

with intricate mosaic floors and colourful wall frescoes, and are set around a lovely courtyard garden.

WORKING ON THE LAND

Behind the villa lies a busy farmyard, with outbuildings around it. There are rooms for the 40 slaves who work on the estate, and sheds for tools and carts.

The stables are here too, housing the oxen

that pull the ploughs, and the donkeys used for carrying loads.

Geese, goats, rabbits and chickens are penned nearby, and there's also a pond full of fish.

It's late summer, and the olives are ripening in the sun. In the farm-yard, the slaves are treading the grapes for wine. The barns are already full of wheat, and the storehouses packed with dried fruits.

Much of this produce will make the long journey from the sunny peace of Tuscany to the noise and dust of Rome. And the next time I'm sipping wine in a street-side bar in town, I shall close my eyes and dream of Tuscany!

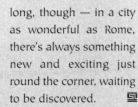

TRADITIONAL GODS ★

Jupiter: chief of all the gods, and the sky god

Juno: chief goddess, goddess of women and of childbirth

Minerva: goddess of wisdom and handicrafts

Mars: god of war

Neptune: god of the sea and all water

Apollo: god of light and healing

Diana: goddess of the moon and also of hunting

Venus: goddess of love and beauty

Saturn: god of growth and farming

Pluto: god of the dead

Mercury: messenger of the gods, and god of merchants

JUPITER   JUNO   MINERVA   DIANA   NEPTUNE

THE BEST GODS?

Illustrated by NICKY COONEY

IT SEEMS AS IF every time our Empire conquers a new country, we learn of a new religion. But how do these foreign cults compare with our traditional gods? *The Roman News* gives both points of view.

"The traditional gods are all we need!" stated the head priest of the god Jupiter, firmly. "Between them, these gods cover every part of our lives — from Juno, the goddess of birth, through to Pluto, the god of the dead.

All of our gods will take good care of us, as long as we show respect for them and keep them happy by offering up prayers and gifts.

And we shouldn't stint on these gifts, either. Pigs, sheep or oxen make the best sacrifices, of course, but offerings of wine, food or money are also well accepted.

CHICKEN FEED

Illustrated by CHRISTIAN HOOK

WHAT KIND OF JOB does an augur do — his main duty is to feed chickens! To find out more, *The Roman News* talked to a member of the College of Augurs.

❓ What is it that you actually do?
Well, you know what it's like when you've got an important decision to make, such as whether to go on a long journey. First of all, you check with the gods to find out if they approve of what you're about to do.

You may go to visit a fortune-teller who throws dice to read the future, or to a diviner who throws bones on the ground and reads the answer from the pattern they make.

But when there are very important decisions to be made, ones that will affect our whole Empire, then the emperor turns to us augurs, his own personal diviners, to consult the gods for him.

❓ So why do you feed chickens?
Well, the gods don't tell us what they think in words — they send us signs instead. My job is to read these signs.

If I scatter grain and the chickens rush to eat it, then I know that the gods are on our side.

MITHRAS   ISIS & SERAPIS   BACCHUS   CYBELE

We should make sure we attend all of the gods' festivals and feasts, too, and the games held in their honour. If we look after our gods, they will look after us.

Of course, every man, woman and child in our Empire should worship the emperor, as well. He does so much for us, he's like a god on Earth.

I simply can't under-stand why any Roman should need to turn to other religions — surely we've enough gods to satisfy everyone!"

MORE LIFE WITH NEW GODS

But when we asked a Roman citizen what he thought, we heard a very different view:

"The traditional gods are so boring! All you have to do is pay for a sacrifice every now and then, and offer up the odd prayer. Where's the excitement in that?

The new cults are a lot more interesting. Take the god Mithras, for example. His followers are all men and, although they're sworn to secrecy, I've heard they meet in dark underground temples to carry out all sorts of dangerous rites. It's no wonder so many of our soldiers follow Mithras.

Then there are Isis and Serapis. Their worshippers have fabulous parades — as good as any theatre.

And as for Bacchus or Cybele, their ceremonies have to be seen to be believed. Their followers get totally drunk or dance themselves into a frenzy. Men and women alike!

What's more, these new gods promise their followers life in the next world, after they die. Now that's something our Roman gods have never offered us!" ✚

But if the chickens don't eat the grain, then it's obvious that the gods don't agree with the emperor's decision. In this case, the emperor would be foolish not to change his plans.

❓ Can anyone become an augur?
No, the emperor himself chooses all the augurs from among the richest and the most important men, the senators.

There are 16 of us augurs, and a new augur is only appointed when one of our number dies.

It's a great honour to be selected. We carry out one of the most important jobs in the Empire — making sure that the gods are behind our great leader and that they support him in his decisions. ✚

GRAINS OF TRUTH: An augur looks for the gods' advice.

WOMEN'S WORK

Illustrated by TUDOR HUMPHRIES

WOMEN OF ROME — it's time to speak your minds! You're always called the weaker sex, best suited to being wives and mothers. But is that how you see yourselves? *The Roman News* asked three different women what they thought of their lives…

SENATOR'S WIFE, 33 years old

"I don't really have time to think much about my life. My husband makes all the major decisions, just as in any marriage. But I'm still responsible for running the household and managing the slaves.

And then there are the children — they're such a handful! I've had eight, and thankfully only three died as babies. I've been lucky myself, too — so many women die in childbirth.

These days, I'm busy teaching my girls the skills they'll need when they marry — spinning, weaving, preparing food, organizing the slaves…

But I do try to find time every day to visit the public baths. And then there are dinner parties or theatre outings with my husband. I don't have time for anything else.

I know some of my friends like talking to their husbands about politics. And they often complain that women don't have any say in how our nation is run — women have never been allowed to vote and we can't go to the law courts.

But as my husband doesn't really approve of women who talk like this, it's just as well that I find politics boring."

BARKEEPER, 24 years old

"Well, I enjoy my life. I'm not married, so I own this bar myself, and there's no man around to tell me what to do!

It's not unusual for a woman to work — lots of women help in their husbands' businesses or run their own shops.

Mind you, it can be hard for a woman to manage a bar. Especially if customers drink too much wine. Then I have to wade in and show them who's the boss!"

VESTAL VIRGIN, 30 years old

"It's not an easy thing, giving your whole life to tending the sacred flame of Vesta, the goddess of the hearth.

We Vestal Virgins leave our families when we're between just 6 and 10 years old. Then we spend the next 30 years living beside the temple. We can't get married.

But I wouldn't want to change my life. Unlike other women, we don't have to obey our fathers' orders. And we're given special honours, like the best seats at the gladiator games. Truly, our position in society is so important that even men treat us with respect."

VESTAL VIRGIN: A life spent tending the sacred flame.

SENATOR'S WIFE: A life spent tending the home.

ON THE THRESHOLD: It's good luck for your new husband to carry you into his house.

CORNELIA'S CORNER
Illustrated by ALAN FRASER

THE ROMAN NEWS' problem page has helped thousands of women over the years. Here are the answers to a few of your typical questions on marriage.

❓ I'm 18 years old and still not married. Is it too late?

It's true, many girls are married by the time they are 12 years old, but not all of us are that lucky! There's still a chance for you to get a husband — if your father can arrange something soon.

❓ I'd like a traditional wedding, but I'm not sure what to do.

Although just moving in with a man counts as getting married — and that's all many women do — a wedding ceremony will show the world that your family is wealthy.

Remember to wear a traditional white tunic, with a flame-coloured veil for your hair.

The day will begin in your father's house, with the marriage ceremonies and a sacrifice to the gods — a pig should be enough. Then there will be a grand feast, paid for by your husband.

Afterwards, you'll set off for your husband's house. It's unlucky to trip as you enter your new home, so make sure your husband carries you over the threshold.

❓ What will happen if I leave my husband?

The good news is that lots of women divorce their husbands, and you won't even need to say why you're doing it. You'll also get back all the money your father gave to your husband when you married.

But there is bad news, too — you *will* have to leave your children with your husband. ◙

ALL ROADS LEAD TO ROME

Illustrated by KATHERINE BAXTER

ROADS HOLD OUR EMPIRE TOGETHER! To govern such vast lands, emperors need to be able to send messages speedily to every town. And soldiers must travel quickly from one area to another in times of trouble.

All this is made possible by the 80,450 kilometres of roads that criss-cross the Empire. *The Roman News* salutes the engineers who created this amazing network, and looks at some of their other building achievements.

CHANNELS: Bringing water.

STONECUTTERS: At work.

ARCHES: Elegant strength.

■ WATER WORKS

Where would we all be without water — no baths, for a start! But how many of us know where our water comes from?

For many towns, the water is brought from rivers high up in the hills. It may flow for hundreds of kilometres, carried by special stone channels called aqueducts.

And where they need to cross valleys, these aqueducts are raised high above the ground on graceful bridges.

Yet these impressive structures would not have been possible if Roman engineers hadn't realized what a strong building shape the arch is!

■ WATER POWER

Not only do our engineers make water flow wherever they want it to, they can even use its power to drive machinery.

Water is channelled through aqueducts to the edge of a steep slope, where it pours straight down over a series of waterwheels.

The force of the water then does all the work — pushing the waterwheels round so they drive the great cogged gearwheels inside the mill building.

And as the gearwheels spin round, they turn the heavy flat stones that grind the flour — that makes the bread, that goes to feed a city!

SURVEYORS: Lining up.

■ RIGHT ON TRACK

The straighter the road, the faster the journey. And our roads aren't just straight, they are well-drained and also very hard-wearing. How do our engineers do it?

First of all, surveyors use special measuring tools to work out the most direct route.

Then soldiers provide all the hard labour. They start by digging a trench into which the road base can be laid. There's often a layer of sand first, then come stone blocks set in cement. Gravel mixed with concrete is next, and the top surface is made up of tough stone slabs or cobbles.

The final touch of genius is to curve the surface so that rainwater flows off it and into the gutters that run down each side of the road.

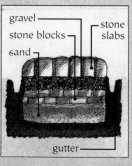

gravel — stone blocks — sand — stone slabs — gutter

ROADS: A stony sandwich.

KEEP CLEAN! ❋ GET FIT! ❋ MEET FRIENDS!

TAKE YOUR DAILY DIP AT CARACALLA'S!

AND RELAX IN THE GLORIOUS WARMTH OF OUR HEATED ROOMS AND POOLS

Illustrated by CHRIS FORSEY

Seven steps to heaven, the Caracalla way

1 First, go to our up-to-date changing rooms, where slaves will help you undress and then oil your skin.

2 Next, have a workout in our modern gymnasium — fully equipped for weight-lifting and ball games.

3 Then scrape off all that oil, sweat and dirt, and head into the tepidarium — our relaxing warm room.

4 Now, dive into our caldarium — a hot room with a hotter pool and the latest in underfloor heating.

5 Most baths leave it at that, but with us you can try the dry heat of the laconicum — guaranteed to sweat away all your tensions.

6 Don't forget to visit our frigidarium for a refreshing plunge in the icy cold pool!

7 And finally, enjoy a relaxing massage from the hands of one of our trained slaves.

And that's not all...
■ Visit our wide range of shops, to buy a new comb or even a slave!
■ Eat a snack in one of our many restaurants.

■ Browse through our well-stocked library.
■ Or simply unwind in our beautiful gardens.

The choice is yours, at the Caracalla Baths!

Open every day:
Women: 10 am – 1 pm
Men: 1 pm – 6 pm

There may be baths in every city in the Empire, but once you've spent a day at the Caracalla Baths in Rome, you'll never want to go anywhere else!

STAYING IN STYLE

Illustrated by SUE SHIELDS

LADIES, ARE YOU fed up with changing fashions? Then let *The Roman News'* style guide help you stand out from the crowd!

✦ CLOTHES

The basic ankle-length tunic never dates, thank goodness. Nor does the elegant stola — although this sleeved over-tunic can only be worn after you're married, of course. And a warm, flowing cloak is best when you take trips outdoors.

But what does make a difference is the colour of your clothes and the fabric you choose.

Many people can only afford garments made of linen or wool, in drab off-white or grey. So if you can manage coloured fabrics, especially if they are silk or cotton, you will be the envy of your less fortunate friends.

The most fashionable colours are blue, red, sea-green, and saffron-yellow. But do avoid purple. It's the height of bad manners to wear this colour unless you belong to the family of either a senator or the emperor.

✦ HAIR

Your hairstyle is another way of getting noticed. The best styles are very elaborate — plaits, twists, ringlets and curls, all piled as high as possible.

But don't risk using an unskilled slave to arrange your hair — it could be disastrous!

Although some women think it looks too bold, blonde is by far the most popular hair colour. If (like most of us) you have dark hair, try bleaching it. Or treat yourself to a blonde wig, but do buy a well-made one.

✦ MAKE-UP

The first rule to looking good is to stay out of the sun. This will keep your skin pale, with no hint of a vulgar suntan.

But if staying indoors is a problem for you, you'll find plenty of skin-whitening pastes and powders in the shops.

Apply a little rouge to give your cheeks a delicate glow, and darken your eyes and eyebrows with soot or crushed ants' eggs. Don't overdo it, though, or you'll end up looking common.

✦ JEWELLERY

Once again, don't wear too much. Rings are fine, as are bracelets, anklets and necklaces. But forget about earrings — they will make you look like a barbarian! ✦

BIG NIGHT OUT: Dress in your best if you want to impress.

WHO'S WEARING THE TROUSERS?

Illustrated by SUE SHIELDS

PICTURE OF POWER: A senator shows off his stripes.

T HE FRENCH DO IT. The Britons do it. Even some of our soldiers do it. But should the rest of us men be wearing trousers? The barbarians claim that they're comfortable and warm. But *The Roman News* still votes for the classic tunic and toga, and here's why!

NOTHING COULD BE easier to wear than a tunic. Just slip it over your head, belt it, and there you are — ready for the day!

It really doesn't matter whether your tunic is made of linen or wool, but keep it knee-length so that it doesn't get in your way. A hard-wearing leather tunic is the best choice for a working man, of course.

And what could be simpler or warmer than a woollen toga? Even youngsters quickly get the hang of arranging this long piece of cloth

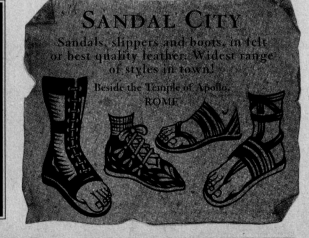

— over the left shoulder, round the back, under the right arm, tucked into your belt and over the left shoulder again.

But the toga is more than a fashion statement. It tells the world you're a citizen, and not a slave.

Just think of all the fuss we make on a boy's 14th birthday — the day when he puts aside the purple-banded toga of childhood for the all-white toga of manhood.

PURPLE POWER!

Of course, the greatest honour of all is given to the men who lead us. How proud our senators must be of the broad purple stripe that edges their togas.

Barbarians just look scruffy in comparison. Their baggy, checked trousers and their rough woollen shirts may be all right for the cold north, but they really shouldn't be worn anywhere else.

So show the world you're a Roman — wear your toga with pride! ✦

Cartoon by MARTIN BROWN

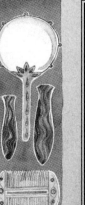

FANTASTIC FEASTS!

Illustrated by RICHARD HOOK

LET *THE ROMAN NEWS* show you how it's done! Follow our ten-step guide to giving the best dinner party ever.

1 STAR GUEST
Everyone wants to meet famous people, so invite someone important — a senator or a general. Then all the other leading citizens will want to come to the party, too.

2 GUESSING GAME
Don't ask anyone else until the day before your dinner party. This will make people even more anxious to attend!

And make all of your guests feel really special by sending your slaves to invite each one of them individually.

3 SWEET SMELLS
Fill your home with the scent of flowers or perfumed oils, so your guests feel relaxed.

When the guests are seated, have your slaves bathe their hands and feet in perfumed water.

4 SITTING COMFORTABLY
Give your guests plenty of room — never try to squash more than three people on to each couch. And don't place any more than three couches around a table.

5 IN THE MOOD
Music is another good way to put your guests at ease. Do make sure you hire professional musicians, though, and ask them to keep the music soft and slow, so that it doesn't drown out the conversation. Flutes and harps are ideal.

6 WISE WINES
You'll probably be offering a choice of wines — spiced, warm, iced, or

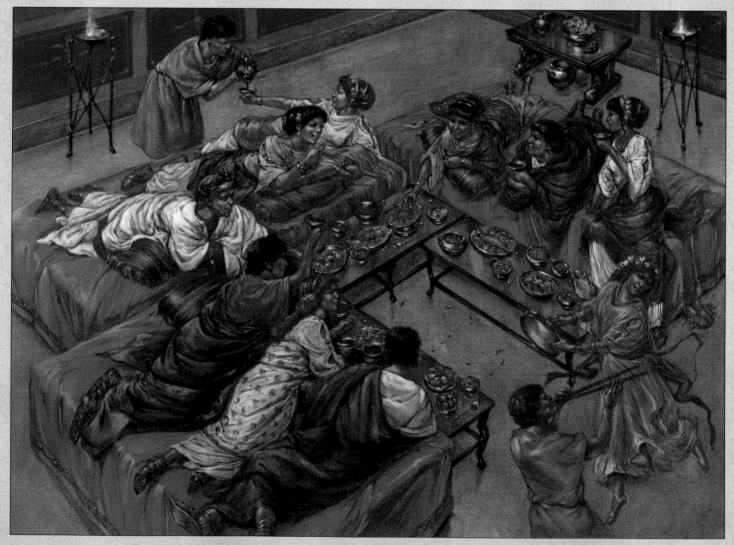

A GREAT NIGHT OUT: Make your party an evening to remember, with fine food and exotic entertainment.

sweetened with honey. But don't spoil the fun by letting people drink too much too soon — mix the wine with water!

7 ONLY THE BEST

You can offer anything from three to ten courses, but the more dishes the better.

Include the usual starters (olives, salads, oysters), but also add something special, such as peahens' eggs.

Follow this up with a selection of fish and meat dishes — stuffed dormice are always popular. And remind your cook to prepare an impressive range of mouth-watering sauces.

Finish off your feast with nuts, fruit and, of course, honey cakes.

8 CENTREPIECE

Make sure you serve your most exotic dish in the middle of the meal. We suggest a flamingo or peacock, a wild boar, or a large tasty fish, such as a sturgeon. Serve the animal in one piece, stuffed with other treats.

9 SICK CARE

There will always be someone who wants more, even when he's full to bursting.

Set aside one room as a vomitorium, so that your guests can be sick quickly and quietly, and then come back to the table to start again.

10 FLOOR SHOW

Hire jugglers, acrobats, conjurers or exotic dancers for your guests' entertainment during and after the meal. We do advise against gladiator fights, though — the blood will make a terrible mess of your room! 🌀

WHAT A DISH!

AMAZE YOUR dinner guests with these fine dishes, from the cookbook of that famous lover of food, Apicius.

BOILED OSTRICH

✦ Make sure the ostrich is properly plucked and cut into large pieces.

✦ Put the pieces into large saucepans, cover with water and simmer.

✦ Make a sauce from pepper, celery seeds, dates, honey, vinegar, mint, fish sauce and oil. Bring to the boil and thicken with cornflour.

✦ Arrange the ostrich so that it looks like a whole bird and cover it with the hot sauce.

SNAIL SNACKS

✦ You will need to prepare your snails a few weeks in advance.

✦ Only choose snails that are good to eat. You'll need about ten for each person. Clean the shells thoroughly.

✦ Let the snails live in a pan of milk until they are fat and juicy.

✦ Fry them in oil and serve hot. 🌀

FREE FOR ALL

EACH EMPEROR BELIEVES that handing out food to the citizens of Rome will make him popular. *The Roman News* talked to a man in the street, to find out what people really think about the emperors' gifts.

WELL, I DON'T know about making emperors popular, but it certainly stops them from getting a knife in the back!

I mean, it's all right for rich folk — they can afford to buy anything they want. Many of them have country farms and grow most of their own food, anyway.

But the rest of us! There are so many people living in Rome these days that farmers just can't grow enough to feed us all.

Half the time you can't even find basic foods like bread and beans, or vegetables and fruit in the shops here, let alone things like fish and meat.

Mind you, meat's so pricey! I just can't afford it often on my wages, I can tell you.

KEEPING THE PEOPLE SWEET

Let's face it, my family would go hungry if it wasn't for the emperor's monthly handouts. We get grain for making bread, as well as olive oil and wine, you know. And they're even giving us pork now.

All this free food is probably costing the emperor a fortune, but there would be riots if he tried to stop it!

And anyway, it's a tradition. Well, it's been going on for hundreds of years, hasn't it — since at least 58 BC.

I say, long live the emperor — well, as long as he carries on lending a helping hand to my family and my mates, that is! 🌀

DOWN WITH SCHOOL!

Illustrated by ANGUS McBRIDE

A WASTE OF TIME! That's what one 12-year-old boy thinks about school. And he's written to *The Roman News*, listing his complaints.

"EVER SINCE my 7th birthday, a slave has taken me to school at the crack of dawn five days a week.

Then I had to sit still all morning, and listen to my schoolteacher droning on, trying to teach me how to count, write and read — not just in our own Latin language, but in Greek, too.

But then after my 11th birthday things got even worse! My 12-year-old sister stopped going to school because she got married, but I was sent to another teacher, called a grammaticus.

Now I have to study poetry and history, as well as the works of great thinkers like Plato. But I can't see the use of any of that old stuff. I have to learn everything off by heart, too, and answer endless questions. And if I make a mistake, my teacher whips me!

Most Roman children of my age don't go to school at all. They work alongside their fathers, learning their trades. Why can't I?"

RIGHT OF REPLY

At *The Roman News* we like to present both sides of a case, so we asked a teacher for his response to the lad's letter.

SOME CHOICE: Children who don't go to school have to work, like this blacksmith's son.

"Well, for a start, this youngster should understand how lucky he is to get any kind of education. Most children don't go to school at all, because their parents can't afford it. His father must be a wealthy man.

What this boy doesn't realize is that it isn't just reading the great Roman and Greek authors that's important — answering questions about their ideas teaches him the art of discussion.

This is the first step in learning how to speak in public — a vital skill if he wants to become a senator or some other politician one day."

So there you are, young man. School will help you to get a good start in life. Keep going to lessons, work hard, and stop grumbling!

JOBS

FOR SALE

✦ **753 BC**
The city of Rome is founded by Romulus.

✦ **509 BC**
The last king is thrown out of Rome and the Roman Republic begins.

✦ **264–202 BC**
Two long wars against the Carthaginians, known as the Punic Wars, end with the city of Carthage under Roman control. The city itself is finally destroyed in 146 BC, in the Third Punic War.

✦ **49–45 BC**
Civil war, which leads to Julius Caesar becoming dictator for life.

✦ **44 BC**
Julius Caesar is murdered.

✦ **42–31 BC**
Further civil wars last until Augustus triumphs at the Battle of Actium.

✦ **27 BC**
Augustus becomes the first emperor — the start of the Roman Empire.

✦ **AD 43**
The conquest of Britain begins. Britain becomes the farthest north that the Empire reaches.

✦ **AD 71**
Emperor Vespasian holds a Triumph to celebrate his victory over rebellious Hebrews in Palestine.

✦ **AD 79**
Pompeii is destroyed when Mount Vesuvius erupts unexpectedly.

✦ **AD 116**
The Empire reaches its greatest extent, under the Emperor Trajan.

✦ **AD 117–138**
Defences of wood and earth are built along the Empire's north-eastern boundaries.

✦ **AD 122**
Hadrian's Wall is begun, in Britain.

✦ **AD 285**
Emperor Diocletian splits the Empire among four co-emperors.

✦ **AD 324**
Constantine reunites the Empire and becomes sole emperor. He founds a new capital in Turkey in AD 326, Constantinople.

✦ **AD 395**
The Empire is divided again, into the Eastern and the Western empires.

✦ **AD 410**
The city of Rome is raided by barbarians, the Visigoths.

✦ **AD 455**
Rome is sacked again, by another barbarian tribe, the Vandals.

✦ **AD 476**
From this date, Italy is controlled by barbarian kings. This is the end of the Western Roman Empire. The Eastern Roman Empire becomes the Byzantine Empire.

Some of the dates in this book have the letters "BC" after them. BC stands for "Before Christ" — so 300 BC, for example, means 300 years before the birth of Christ.

If the letters "AD" appear in front of the date, the event happened after the birth of Christ.

The Ancient Romans did not count time in this way.

In this book, many of the country names are the ones we use today, such as France or Syria. The Ancient Romans would have used different names.

Author: Andrew Langley
Consultant:
Philip de Souza
St Mary's University
College,
University of Surrey
Editor: Lesley Ann Daniels
Designer: Beth Aves

Advert illustrations by:
Katherine Baxter: 19br
Nicky Cooney: 11tl,
27bl, 31
Maxine Hamil: 18br,
27br, 30bl
Matthew Lilly: 19bl
Robbie Polley: 18bl
Sue Shields: 23bl
Tony Smith: 23ml, 30br
Mike White: 23tl, 26

Decorative borders by:
John Le Brocq: 1bm
Nicky Cooney: 13tr, 26
Maxine Hamil: 1, 9, 17, 19,
20 and 21, 29
Sue Shields: 22

With thanks to:
Linden Artists Ltd, Pennant
Illustration Agency,
Temple Rogers Artists'
Agents, Virgil Pomfret
Artists Agency Ltd.

First published 1996 by
Walker Books Ltd
87 Vauxhall Walk
London SE11 5HJ

This edition
published 2000

2 4 6 8 10 9 7 5 3

Text © 1996
Andrew Langley

Illustrations © 1996
Walker Books Ltd

Printed in
Hong Kong

British Library
Cataloguing in
Publication Data

A catalogue record for
this book is available
from the British Library.

ISBN 0-7445-7713-6

IMPORTANT ROMAN EMPERORS AND THEIR DATES OF RULE

✦ **Augustus**, first emperor   27 BC–AD 14

✦ **Claudius**, won new   AD 41–54
lands for the Empire

✦ **Nero**, tyrannical emperor,   AD 54–68
committed suicide

✦ **Vespasian**, built the   AD 69–79
Colosseum

✦ **Trajan**, extended the   AD 98–117
Empire in the East

✦ **Hadrian**, built strong   AD 117–138
borders to the Empire

✦ **Diocletian**, divided the   AD 284–305
Empire between four
different rulers

✦ **Constantine**, reunited   AD 306–337
the Empire

✦ **Romulus Augustus**, last   AD 475–476
emperor of the Western
Roman Empire